BEPO

BEPO IS A BREAD & BUTTER GUIDE TO THIS CRAZY THING CALLED LIFE.

IT IS A SHORT, TO THE POINT REFERENCE BOOK FOR ANY HUMAN,
BIG OR SMALL ON THE DAY TO DAY ATTITUDES AND MINDSET WE FEEL
WILL STAND YOU IN GOOD STEAD IN YOUR FUTURE.

WHATEVER YOUR AGE, CREED, RELIGION .

THESE SIMPLE PAGES OF BEPOLOGY
AIM TO SPUR YOU ON TO BE THE BEST
YOU CAN BE IN WHATEVER YOU DO.

WE ARE BEPO

ENJOY

ATTITUDE:YOU NEED A GOOD ONE

ASPIRATIONS:HAVE THEM, THINK BIG

ABILITY:ALSO KNOWN AS HARD WORK

ACHIEVE(MENTS):THESE WILL HAPPEN

ANYONE CAN:JUST REMEMBER THIS SIMPLE FACT. LITERALLY ANYONE CAN DO ANYTHING

BE POSITIVE:THIS IS A GAME CHANGER!
THINK & DO GOOD STUFF

BE THE BEST YOU CAN BE:IN ALL YOU DO, DAILY

BELIEF:HAVE THIS IN ABUNDANCE. IF YOU BELIEVE IN
YOU OTHERS WILL. FACT

BREAD & BUTTER:MAKE WHAT YOU DO YOURS.
DO THE BASICS RIGHT. REST WILL FOLLOW

BE YOU:NO GIMMICKS, NO LIES

BE FREE:THERE ARE NO CONSTRAINTS IN THIS LIFE UNLESS YOU MAKE THEM

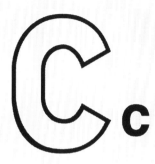

Cc

CREATIVITY:BE CREATIVE, USE THAT BRAIN OF YOURS WISELY

CONFIDENCE:THIS COMES WITH TIME & PRACTICE,
HONE YOUR CRAFT

COLLABORATE:MIX IT UP WITH AS MANY
HUMANS AS POSSIBLE, HUMANS KNOW STUFF

CHALLENGE:YOURSELF DAILY, THIS LIFE IS NOT SUPPOSED
TO BE EASY. WORK HARD

Dd

DEVELOP:YOURSELF, HARNESS WHAT YOU CREATE,
DEVELOP WHATEVER 'IT' IS INTO SOMETHING GREAT

DO:NOT SHY AWAY FROM ANYTHING

DARE:TO BE DIFFERENT,
IT'S NOT ALL ABOUT THE MAINSTREAM

DO GOOD STUFF

DETERMINATION:A LIFE SKILL
WHICH WILL PROVE INVALUABLE

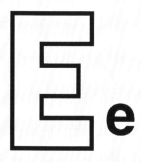

E e

ENJOY YOURSELF:WISE WORDS
FROM NANNA HILDA & PRINCE BUSTER

EXPLORE:THIS CRAZY PLANET

EXPERIENCE EVERYTHING

EDUCATE:YOUR BRAIN

ENHANCE:YOUR MIND

EVOLVE:INTO YOUR OWN SKIN

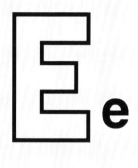

FOCUS:YOUR MIND

FUN:SOMETHING YOU NEED DAILY

FAMILY:UNFORTUNATELY NOT YOUR CHOICE!
THIS IS WHAT MAKES YOU, YOU.

FRIENDS:CHOOSE WISELY,
THE BEST ONES ARE FOREVER

FRESH AIR:GET OUTSIDE, COME RAIN OR SHINE,
BREATHE,
KEEP FIT, IT'S GOOD FOR YOU

FAILURE:THIS WILL HAPPEN, HAVE NO FEAR AS
THIS BUILDS CHARACTER
AND WILL FOCUS YOU ON YOUR FUTURE

G g

GROW:IN STATURE & KNOWLEDGE,
FEED YOURSELF & YOUR BRAIN

GOAL:SET THESE DAILY.
INSTIL A LONG TERM ONE.
NOT JUST ONE IN THE BACK
GARDEN FOR A KICK ABOUT!

A LIFE GOAL:USE THAT FOCUS TO ACHIEVE THIS

GRAVITATE:YOURSELF TOWARDS THIS DAILY

GUIDANCE:TAKE IT & LEARN FROM IT,
KNOW WHAT IS RIGHT & WRONG

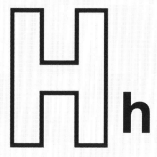

Hh

HELP:YOURSELF & OTHERS

HELP! 'THE BEATLES' A MUST LISTEN.

HIDE:THIS IS NOT AN OPTION.
DO NOT SHY AWAY FROM
ANYTHING YOU FEEL PASSIONATE ABOUT.
YOU WILL BE A BETTER HUMAN FOR THIS. FACT

HARNESS:YOUR SKILLS

BE HAPPY:ALWAYS WEAR A SMILE

HUMAN:REMEMBER, THE MAJORITY OF US ARE HUMAN.
DO NOT BE SCARED OF TREATING PEOPLE AS SUCH.
WE ARE ALL THE SAME.
LARGER BANK ACCOUNTS OR LIVING ON THE STREETS.
TREAT PEOPLE AS YOU WOULD LIKE TO BE TREATED.
THE REST IS DOWN TO THEM. NOT YOU

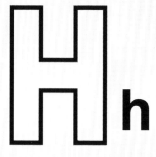

Ii

IDEAS:HAVE THEM.HAVE 100's OF THEM.
WRITE THEM DOWN!.
SOME OF THE SIMPLEST
IDEAS ARE THE GREATEST

INSPIRE:TAKE & GIVE INSPIRATION
TO ANYTHING OR ANYONE YOU CAN

IMAGINE:YOUR FUTURE,
ALSO LISTEN TO A BLOKE CALLED JOHN LENNON'S
SONG CALLED 'IMAGINE' .
POIGNANT TO SAY THE LEAST!

INCLUSION:YES, YOU NEED YOUR OWN SPACE & TIME
BUT, INCLUDE YOURSELF WITH OTHERS.
SHARE YOUR IDEAS,
DEVELOP THEM INTO SOMETHING INSPIRATIONAL

i

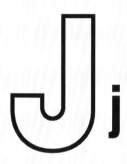

Jj

JOKE:DON'T TAKE MUNDANE,
NON IMPORTANT 'THINGS' TOO SERIOUS
LIFE IS TOO SHORT

JOIN IN:AS MUCH AS YOU CAN. IT BUILDS CHARACTER

JOURNEY:TREAT LIFE AS ONE. KEEP LEARNING.
BE EXCITED,
DARE TO GO AND DO THINGS WHERE OTHERS WOULDN'T

JUDGE:YOU WILL BE JUDGED ON YOUR ACTIONS,
NOT YOUR WORDS. REMEMBER THIS

Kk

KEEP THE FAITH:A SIMPLE YET BEAUTIFUL
MANTRA FROM NORTHERN SOUL DAYS.

KEEP GOING:TO KEEP WHAT YOU HAVE YOU MUST
DO THIS & NEVER GIVE UP.
YOU MUST BE RELENTLESS IN THIS WORLD.

LEARN:FROM WHATEVER & WHOEVER YOU CAN

LISTS:MAKE THEM,IT KEEPS YOU ON TRACK

LOVE:LIFE ITSELF

LAUGH:WHEN THIS HAPPENS SEROTONIN IS
PRODUCED IN YOUR BRAIN, NATURALLY.
THIS IS GOOD STUFF.
LAUGH A LOT,
TOMMY COOPER USUALLY HELPS!

LIVE:THERE ARE MORE THAN ENOUGH HOURS IN A
DAY FOR YOU TO ACHIEVE WORLD DOMINATION,
RUN YOUR OWN BUSINESS,
STUDY FOR TESTS AND LIVE A FRUITFUL, HEALTHY LIFE.
MAKE TIME
TO LIVE NOT JUST EXIST

LISTEN:WITH INTENT, SOMETIMES
IT IS ONLY NECESSARY TO LISTEN & NOT TO TALK

LISTEN ALSO TO MUSIC:IT IS AFTER ALL, THE ANSWER

Mm

MAKE A PLAN:BE READY

MINDSET:A POSITIVE ONE GOES A LONG WAY

MOTIVATION:MAKE IT HAPPEN

MENTALITY:THE RIGHT ONE
WILL TAKE YOU WHEREVER
YOU WANT IN LIFE

MUSIC: AS STATED PREVIOUSLY.
      IT IS THE ANSWER .

Nn

NEVER GIVE UP: EVER

NURTURE:ALL THINGS GOOD,
KEEP THEM CLOSE

NETWORK:YOU HAVE TO BE IN
IT TO WIN IT, GET INTO THE CIRCLES
THAT WILL SATISFY YOUR GOAL

NEGATIVE:DON'T WASTE YOUR TIME
OR ENERGY ON ANYTHING NEGATIVE,
PEOPLE OR THINGS.
NOT GOOD STUFF

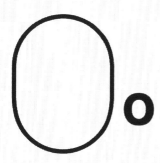

OPPORTUNITY:TAKE IT,MAKE IT,
DON'T SQUANDER IT

OPEN DOORS:DO THE ABOVE AND
THESE WILL BE READILY AVAILABLE.
IF YOU DO GOOD STUFF &
WORK HARD ENOUGH

ORIGINALITY:THIS WILL STAND
YOU OUT FROM THE CROWD.

OASIS:A LITTLE KNOWN UK BAND DID ALL OF THE
ABOVE FROM NOTHING.
HARD WORK & BELIEF,
GREAT SONGS, PASSION & DRIVE. FACT

Pp

POSITIVITY:THIS GOOD ATTITUDE
AND MINDSET WILL HELP YOU ENDLESSLY

PROSPER:SOMETHING THAT WILL HAPPEN IF THE
ABOVE IS APPLIED CORRECTLY

BEING PRODUCTIVE:YOU WILL NEED
TO EXCEL IN THIS TIME
& TIME AGAIN TO GET WHERE YOU WANT TO BE

PERSEVERANCE:PROBABLY
THE ONE CHARACTERISTIC
THAT BRINGS THIS BOOK TOGETHER.
WHATEVER YOUR PATH, WORK @ IT, STICK WITH IT,
IT WILL HAPPEN

PS:NOT A BAD CONCEPT FOR A BRAND EITHER??!!

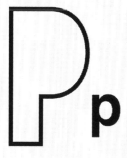

QUALITY:TIME WITH GOOD PEOPLE & FAMILY

QUESTIONS:ALWAYS ASK THEM.
NO SUCH THING AS A STUPID ONE.

QUALIFICATIONS:DEFINITELY NOT ESSENTIAL
BUT WORK HARD AT SCHOOL REGARDLESS.
START AS YOU MEAN TO GO ON

R r

READ:EVERYTHING YOU CAN

RESPECT:YOURSELF & OTHERS

REST:YOU NEED THIS TO SUCCEED

**S**s

SKILLS:LEARN & UTILISE THEM WELL

SCARED:DON'T BE, YOU'LL DO GREAT

SECRETS:TRY NOT TO HAVE ANY.
THEY WILL ARISE AT SOME POINT.
FOR THE GOOD THE BAD OR THE UGLY.

T t

TEST:YOURSELF DAILY

TRUST:YOURSELF AND A LIMITED AMOUNT OF
OTHERS ONCE THEY HAVE EARNED IT

TRAIN:GET GOOD AT STUFF,
PRACTICE THAT STUFF.
ALSO A PRETTY DECENT FORM OF TRANSPORT.

TRY:NEW STUFF

TRAVEL:ANYWHERE & EVERYWHERE,
IT WILL OPEN YOUR MIND

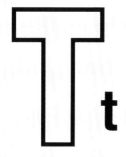

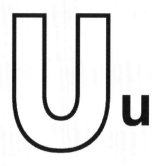

Uu

UTILISE:ALL YOUR
SURROUNDINGS.
YOUR PEERS,
TEACHERS,BOOKS,
FAMILY, INTERNET

V
v

VISUALISE:YOURSELF DOING
WHATEVER IT IS YOU PLAN,
DREAM, WORK FOR

Ww

WORK:HARD, SMART & TO THE BEST OF YOUR ABILITY, ALWAYS

WRITE STUFF DOWN

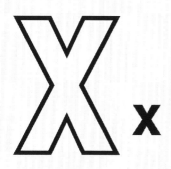

X x

XPRESS YOURSELF: NWA. MASTERPIECE

TAKE TIME TO LISTEN TO THIS

X x

Yy

YOU:LOOK AFTER YOU, MAKE SURE YOU,
CAN BE THE BEST,
YOU , YOU CAN BE.

YOU ARE IN CONTROL

Z z

BEPO

@BEPOSITIVETAYLOREDBRAND

 @TEAMPOSITIVITEE

 @BEPOSITIVE_TAYLOREDBRAND

 BEPOSITIVETAYLOREDBRAND

ALPHABET WITH ATTITUDE IS FOR
YOU.

WHOEVER YOU ARE, WHATEVER YOU DO.

BEPO HQ REALISE THERE ARE MANY, MANY MORE WORDS,
PHRASES, TO KEEP YOU
ON TRACK TO DO GOOD STUFF.

BEPO NOTES IS FOR YOU

USE THEM, ADD YOUR OWN VOCABULARY, YOUR OWN INSPIRATIONS.

ADD YOUR THOUGHTS, YOUR IDEAS, SKETCH YOUR DESIGNS .

STICK WITH IT, TREAT IT NOT AS A DIARY BUT A WAY OF LIFE.

WELCOME TO TEAM BEPO

Printed in Poland
by Amazon Fulfillment
Poland Sp. z o.o., Wrocław

61903167R00066